IRISH GHOST STORIES

GW00982606

Irish Ghost Stories

PATRICK F. BYRNE

THE MERCIER PRESS

The Mercier Press Limited
4 Bridge Street, Cork
24 Lower Abbey Street, Dublin 1

First Published 1965
Reprinted 1968, 1969, 1973, 1975, 1977,
1980, 1984, 1987

This edition 1991

ISBN O 85342 970 7

Printed in Ireland by Colour Books Ltd., Dublin.

Contents

*For Aidan Pender who started the ghosts column
and made this book possible*

Acknowledgments

I wish to thank Independent Newspapers Ltd. and Mr. Aidan Pender, Editor, 'Evening Herald', for permission to use material which has already appeared in the 'Evening Herald' Ghosts Column. Also the following for either relating to me or allowing me to use their stories – Dr. Michael MacLiammoir, the late Mr. Robert Brennan, Sir Shane Leslie, Mr. Denis Brennan, Miss Maire O'Donnell, Mrs. E. M. Thompson, Dun Laoghaire; Mr. F. W. Gumley, Glasnevin; Mr. J. Hayes of Clontarf; Mrs. K. Callery of Kilkenny; Mrs. Violet Smyth of Roundwood; Mr. Patrick J. Donaghy; Garda Sergeant James Lowe, Mr. Liam Shine, Mr. David O. Watson of Belfast; Mr. S. Stevenson of Belfast, Miss C. Mac-Mullen Tivy of Adambeg, Midleton, Co. Cork; Mr. H. M. B. of Rochfortbridge, Co. Westmeath; Mr. J. S. B. of Lanesboro, Co. Longford; Mr. Patrick Stewart of Patrickswell, Limerick; Mr. Noel Smith, Limerick Mrs. M. E. Thompson Castlegarde and Mr. Teddy Aherne, Herne Hill, London.

In addition, I wish to acknowledge the permission to quote from the following books.

The Silent Years by John Francis Byrne (Cranly and the Haunted House on Cork Hill) by permission of the publishers, Farrar, Straus & Company, Inc., copyright 1953 by J. F. Byrne.

True Irish Ghost stories compiled by St. John D. Seymour B.D. Litt. D. and Harry L. Neligan D.I.R.I.C. by permission of Messrs. Hodges Figgis & Co. Ltd.

Malachy Horan remembers by George A. Little. Extracts reprinted by permission of the author and the publishers.

Myself and Others by Annie M. P. Smithson. Extracts by permission of the Talbot Press.

Window on Maynooth by Dennis Meehan. Extract by permission of the author and Messrs. Clonmore and Reynolds.

I would also like to thank my wife for her excellent co-operation by doing all the typing and helping to put the book together.

CHAPTER 1

In History's Pages

On the first day of May (Bealtaine) the Tuatha de Danaan landed in North-West Connacht, legend has it, and the Firbolgs who were in Ireland before them, did not see them landing as the hills and coast were covered by a fairy mist. In Ireland the fairy mist they brought with them seems to have stayed, if one is to judge by the strange happenings recorded over the centuries. Ghosts, in the modern sense were unknown to pre-Christian Ireland. In those days it was the old Pagan Gods that were reported as appearing to people.

Their headquarters were at Brugh no Boinne on the banks of the Boyne, where the Dagda, the 'Red Man of all Knowledge' had his home; in the Boyne itself lived the Dagda's son, the handsome Angus, who guarded young lovers, and who was seen by many of the Kings at Tara, including the great Cormac Mac Art.

Near Tara also lived that terrifying Goddess of Battles, the Morrigu. Her appearance always signified the horror of things to come — the screams of men dying in battle, homes burned to the ground, the wailing of women. She appeared to Cuchulain and spoke to him just before his heroic death at the Pillar Stone in Louth.

And, of course, there was Midhir and Etain, the immortal lovers who died, were born again and met in the Great Hall of the King's Palace at Tara, they recognised one another and flew away together as swans – a story which has been beautifully woven into a play in a modern setting by Michael MacLiammoir.

Lastly, there was Manannan Mac Lir, the proud and angry Ocean God, as the poem tells us... 'whose angry lips, in their white foam full often did inter, whole fleets of ships.'

In the Fianna Cycle there are tales of the appearance of beautiful men and women from Tir-na-nOg; palaces that appear and disappear (the Fairy Palace of the Quicken Trees, for example) and in one story Fionn Mac Cumhaill meets a handscome young man who turns out to be himself when young.

With the coming of St. Patrick the supernatural events recorded generally involved demons and the spirits of evil who troubled the hermits in their solitude and the monks in their monasteries. In pre-Christian days when hero battled with hero, now it became a wrestling match between good and evil, the holy men and the devils. The beautiful young woman from Tir-na-nOg became the Bean Sidhe, or Fairy Woman, and her arrival was to announce the death of a member of some ancient clan.

Fionn Mac Cumhaill and the leaders of the Fianna were said to be sleeping, with their weapons by their side under the Hill of Allen waiting to hear the shrill of the trumpet, the Dord Fiann calling them to defend their country from the invader, and this brings us to the story of Garrett Og Firzgerald, the Eleventh Earl of Kildare.

Garrett Og died in London on sixteenth of November, 1585, and his body was brought back to Ireland and interred in St. Brigid's Cathedral, Kildare. He was known as 'The Wizard Earl' because he was said to practice the black art. He was able to change himself into other shapes, such as bird or beast, and as a result of this became a terror to the countryside.

His wife, the Countess, had never seen him practise these strange wings as he used to retire to a secret room in the castle. She frequently begged him to transform himself before her, but this he refused to do. He said that if he did, and she became afraid, he would be taken from her, and never be seen again.

She kept on asking, however, until in the end he agreed to do as she wished, but first she must undergo three trials to test her courage. In the first trial the River Grees, which flowed past the castle walls, over-flowed its banks at a sign from the Earl and flooded the banqueting hall where they were standing. The Countess remained undisturbed.

At the Earl's command the waters receded, and the second test began. A hugh eel-like monster appeared at one of the windows, slid through, crawled about among the furniture, and finally coiled itself around the body of the Countess. Still she showed no fear, and at a nod from the Earl the creature uncoiled itself and dis-appeared.

In the third test an intimate friend of hers long since dead entered the room and passing slowly by went out at the other end. The Countess showed not the slightest fear, and the Earl was satisfied that he could trust her, but again warned her of the danger if she became afraid when he changed his shape.

He then turned himself into a large black bird, flew about the room and perching on the Countess's shoulder began to sing. Suddenly a black cat appeared and made a spring at the bird; the Countess forgot the warning and fearing for the bird's safety, threw up her arms and fainted. When she came to she was alone, the bird and the cat had disappeared, and she never saw the Earl again!

It was said that the Earl and his Knights lie in an enchanted sleep, their horses beside them, in a cave under the Rath of Mullaghmast, about five miles north of Kilkea Castle. Once in seven years they come out, gallop around the Curragh and then across the country to Kilkea Castle where they enter the haunted wing, and then return to the Rath of Mullaghmast.

The Earl was said to be mounted on a white charger shod with silver shoes, and when those shoes were worn out the enchantment would be broken, and he would come out, drive the English from Ireland, and reign again over the vast estates of his ancestors. Shortly before 1798 he was said to have been seen by a blacksmith who was crossing the Curragh in a cart from Athgarvan to Kildare. He was asked to examine the horse's shoes but they were not yet worn out.

Another legend said that late one evening a farmer was returning from a fair in Athy. He was going in the direction of Ballytore and when passing near the Rath of Mullaghmast was astonished to see a bright light coming from it. On going closer he noticed that the light came from a cave in which several men in armour were asleep with their horses beside them.

Cautiously he crept up to the entrance, and seeing that neither man nor beast stirred he grew bolder and entered the cave; he examined the saddlery on the horses, and the mens armour and plucking up courage slowly began to draw a sword from its sheath, as he did so the owner's head began to arise and he heard a voice say in Irish – 'Has the time come?' In terror, as he let go of the sword, the farmer replied 'No, sir,' and fled from the place.

It was said that if the farmer had completely unsheathed the sword the enchantment would have been broken and the Earl would have come into his own again.

Lord Tyrone and Lady Beresford

One of the most famous of Irish ghost stories is that concerning Lord Tyrone (John Le Poer) and Lady Beresford (Nichola Sophia Hamilton). They were orphans and were reared by an atheistic guardian who tried to enforce his views upon them. As a result of this the two young people made a vow that the first to die should appear to the other if there was a life beyond the grave.

In the course of time Nichola Hamilton married Sir Tristram Beresford. One night she awoke in terror to find her foster-brother standing beside the bed. He bade her be quiet, and told her he had just died and reminded her of the vow made years before. He told her of many future things including the death of her husband. He also said that she would marry again, have four more children and that soon after the birth of her last one, on the day of her forty-seventh birthday her own death would take place.

Having heard all this Lady Beresford asked how would she know that it was not all a dream. At this Lord Tyrone took her wrist in his icy clasp, and immediately it shrank and withered. For the remainder of her life she always wore a black silk ribbon over the deformity.

All the predictions came to pass up to the birth of her fourth child by her second marriage. Despite this she reached her forty-eigth birthday, and decided to celebrate the occasion with a few friends. One of those invited was a clergyman, an old friend of her family.

'I am 48 today,' she told him with delight. To her dismay the clergyman said – 'No, you are mistaken. You are only 47.'

Shaking and pale, Lady Beresford asked – 'Are you sure?' The clergyman said he was positive, as he had been looking at the register only a few days before.

'Then you have signed my death warrant,' she said. She retired to her room made her will and died later that night. The house in which the ghostly pact was made was said to have been Gill Hall, Co. Down, the 367-acre estate which was sold a few years ago.

Clongowes Wood near Clane, Co. Kildare, was once the home of the Eustace family, who forfeited it for their part in the Insurrection of 1641. It then passed into the hands of Richard Reynel, who in 1667 sold it to the Brownes. One of this family later became a Marshal in the Austrian Army, and while he was serving in the wars the house was occupied by his two sisters.

One afternoon the ladies were engaged with their needlework in a room off the hall when to their amazement they saw their brother come in in his full regimental uniform. He held his hands against his breast and there were red stains on his tunic. The ladies followed him up the stairs but on reaching one of the bedrooms the figure vanished.

Convinced that the apparition foretold the death of the Marshall the good ladies immediately went into mourning and had Masses offered for his soul. They even held a 'wake' which was attended by the local gentry. Several weeks later an official letter arrived at the house telling of the Marshal's death at the Battle of Prague.

Charles Fort

Charles Fort, a former British military station near Kinsale, which was erected in 1667 by the Duke of Ormonde was said to be haunted by the ghost of the 'White Lady'. The story behind this is as follows:

Shortly after the fort was built Colonel Warrender, a strict disciplinarian, was appointed its governor. He had a daughter named 'Wilful' who fell in love with and married Sir Trevor Ashurst. On the evening of their wedding day, as the happy couple were walking along the battlements of the fort, the bride saw some flowers growing on the rocks beneath. She expressed a wish for them, and a sentry posted close by volunteered to climb down to get them if Sir Trevor took his place during his absence.

Sir Trevor agreed, and took the soldier's greatcoat and musket while the latter went in search of a rope, and began his descent. Meantime, Sir Trevor, overcome by the excitement of the day, fell asleep. Along came the governor, making his customary rounds of the sentries and challenged the sleeping man. Receiving no answer, and realising the sentry was asleep on duty, the angry governor drew his pistol and shot him trough the heart!

It was only on inspecting the body that he realised his mistake. When the young bride learned what had happened she rushed distractedly from the house and flung herself over the battlements. In despair at the double tragedy her father shot himself during the night.

The 'White Lady' is the ghost of the young bride. Major Black who was attached to the Fort, and served in the Peninsular War reported seeing the wraith in the early years of the nineteenth century. He used see the figure passing up and down the stairs. In 1880 Captain Marvell Hull and Lieut. Hartland were going from room to room in the fort when on a landing they were

18

confronted by a woman in a white dress. She turned and looked towards them showing a beautiful, but colourless face, and then passed on through a locked door.

On one occasion in the same fort some officers found themselves flung down the stairs by an invisible force.

Wallstown Castle

A rather curious apparition was said to haunt Wallstown Castle in Co. Cork, the seat of the Wall family. The castle was burned down by the Cromwellian troops in 1642 and Colonel Wall, the head of the family, was captured, and imprisoned in Cork Jail where he died. One of the defenders during the siege was a man named Henry Bennett, who was killed while fighting. His ghost was said to be seen around the ruins after his death.

He wore the Cavalier dress of the period with a white hat and in his hand he carried a pole which he used to place across the road near the castle to stop travellers; on being asked to withdraw it, he would do so and laugh heartily. A man who lived in a cottage in the vicinity used to report that the apparition often came to his window and pushed the pole through. When asked to withdraw it he would do so with an accompanying hollow laugh.

CHAPTER 2

In old Dublin

Marsh's Library

In a quiet corner of old Dublin, beside St. Patrick's Cathedral stands Marsh's Library, the first public library in Ireland. Originally the private library of Archbishop Narcissus Marsh (1638–1713) whose Palace is now the Garda Depot in Kevin Street, it still retains its old-world atmosphere.

About 50 years ago the library was said to be haunted by the ghost of its founder. He was reported to frequent the inner gallery which contained his favourite books. It was said that he moved in and out among the cases taking down some of the volumes from the shelves and occasionnally throwing them down on the reader's desk as if in anger. In the morning things were always found to be in order.

The story behind this was that the Archbishop reared one of his nieces from childhood and loved her like his own daughter. The niece fell in love and eloped with a foreign sea captain whose boat was moored at the end of Winetavern Street. Before doing so, however, she wrote a note to her uncle asking his forgiveness, and placed it in one of his favourite books. The Archbishop never found it in his lifetime, and so his ghost is said to be still seeking it.

When the library was first opened to the public the books were chained to the shelves and readers were searched on the way out to see if they had a precious volume under their great-coat. The chains and locks may still be seen. Those were the days before one could bring a book home from the library to read in comfort before a blazing fire.

Dean Swift was a frequent visitor to the library and his caustic comments may be read in the margins of some of the books, so perhaps it might be that the ghost is that of the great satirist trying to obliterate some of his uncharitable scribblings.

The connecting door between the library and the Palace may still be seen. When the latter first became a police barracks last century many of the then Dublin Metropolitan Police reported strange happenings, such as noises and figures been seen in the dormitories. Nothing has been reported in recent years, but the courtyard is still a rather spooky place on a dark winter's evening.

Marshalsea Barracks

The Marshalsea Barracks in Bridgefoot Street, Dublin was originally built about 200 years ago as a Debtors's Prison, but in 1798 was taken over by the military during the Rising. A large number of captured insurgents were taken there and tortured beefore execution. One of them, Pat Doyle, a Wexfordman, made a desperate effort to escape.

A powerfully built fellow, he overpowered three of the guards, and managed to scale the thirty-foot wall. When he had reached the top, however, he lost his footing, and tumbled to his death in the backyard of a house in Bridgefoot Street. For years afterwards many people claimed to have seen his ghost prowling along the top of the wall, seeking a way to escape.

The Marshalsea was taken over by the Corporation in 1932 and converted into flats. A vast new scheme of flats is now beside it.

Lord Norbury

John Toler, better known as Lord Norbury, the Hanging Judge, who presided at the trial of Robert Emmet and many of the '98 leaders lived in a big house in Cabra, Dublin. Until the house was pulled down just before the war there were all sorts of ghost stories told about it. One of these was that the bloodthirsty judge on his death was changed into a phantom black dog whose fate was for eternity to prowl around the area at night, dragging a large chain behind him.

Another story about Norbury was that he once wrongfully convicted a young married man from Blanchardstown, Co. Dublin of sheep-stealing, a capital crime in those days, and the man wat later hanged. His widow went into a decline, and died soon after him. On her death-bed she cursed the Judge and vowed that whether she came back from Heaven or Hell she would never let Norbury have an unbroken night's sleep in his own house. As a result he was said to suffer from chronic insomnia.

The house was demolished just before the war to make way for the new housing estates in Cabra West.

In the winter of 1840–41 a skating party was enjoying itself on the pond in the grounds of the Castle near Rathfarnham, Co. Dublin. Among the skaters was a man who had with him a very fine curly-coated retriever dog.

The pond was thronged with people enjoying themselves, when suddenly the ice gave way beneath him, and the man fell into the water; the dog went to his rescue, and both were drowned. A monument was later erected to perpetuate the memory of the dog's heroic self-sacrifice. The ghost of the dog was said to have haunted the grounds and the public road between the Castle Gate and the Dodder Bridge. Many people were said to have seen the dog, and the story is well known locally.

The ghost of a boy who was murdered by a Romany was said to have haunted one of the lodge gates of the Castle demesne. The Castle, has been in the possession of the Jesuit Fathers and there has been no sign of a ghost there for a long time now.

Law case

A law case about a haunted house took place in Dublin in 1885. A Mr. Waldron, a solicitor's clerk, sued his next-door neighbour, one Mr. Kiernan, a mate in the merchant service, to recover £500 for damages done to his house. Kiernan denied the charges, but asserted that Waldron's house was haunted. Witnesses proved that every night, from August 1884 to January 1885, stones were thrown at the windows and doors, and extraordinary and inexplicable occurrences constantly took place.

Mrs. Waldron, wife of the plaintiff, swore that one night she saw one of the panes of glass of a certain window cut through with a diamond, and a white hand inserted through the hole. She at once caught up a bill-hook and aimed a blow at the hand, cutting off one of the fingers. This finger could not be found, nor were any traces of blood seen.

A servant of hers, she said, was persecuted by noises and the sound of footsteps. Mr. Waldron, with the aid of detectives and policeman, endeavoured to find out the cause, but with no success. The witnesses in the case were closely cross-examined, but without shaking their testimony. The facts appeared to be proved, so the jury found for Kiernan, the defendant. At least twenty people had testified on oath to the fact that the house had been known to have been haunted.

Dublin Cathedral

About 60 years ago the following report appeared in the Dublin Evening Herald: 'An extraordinary story is going the rounds of the Dublin clergy. It is stated that a lady who is in the habit of attending one of our cathedrals has lately seen the figure of a deceased member of the Chapter sitting in his place in the choir. To add to the mystery, one of the members of the staff of the cathedral has asserted that a similar appearance of the same person has occurred to her. The story is told by a dignitary of the city who himself is regarded as no mean authority on such mysteries.'

The Widow Gammon

Near Monkstown, Co. Dublin is the Widow Gammon's Hill which is said to be haunted by the 'Widow's' ghost. The story behind it is as follows: A monastery stood in the area as local place names indicate, in pre-Reformation days. By the time of Cromwell the monks were still hiding out in local farmhouses. The Widow Gammon is said to have informed on them to the soldiers and they were caught and put to death.

When the widow herself died, her spirit was said to be seen on occasions afterwards at the place where the monks had been caught. One local man claimed he had seen her, and that she had placed her hand on his neck and burned him, leaving a scar for life.

'An old friend of mine living in the Monkstown area for over 80 years, told us never to go near the Widow's Hill after midnight as he and several of his friends had seen her there,' writes Mrs. E. M. Thompson, Dun Laoghaire. 'There is a very old graveyard nearby. My friend tells me that years ago, he and a brother were driving home long after midnight, when passing this graveyard they saw the Widow come out. She locked the iron gate and then turned, flashed a great iron key at them and disappeared.'

'About three years after this the same two men saw her again coming out of an old ruined castle. She held a shining article the shape of an axe in one hand and the key in the other. She crossed the road swiftly from the old castle and unlocked the graveyard gate and passed through.'

'Years later my friends saw the Widow once more, this time walking slowly up and down the graveyard path again with the axe shining in her hand.'

Oldbawn

In the seventeenth century Archdeacon Bulkeley lived in Oldbawn House outside Tallaght, Co. Dublin. A story current in the area until recent years was that his ghost was to be seen in a coach drawn by six headless horses from his house to other parts of his vast estate.

CHAPTER 3

Dublin... after 1900

Cranly and the haunted house of Cork Hill

One of the best ghost stories about Dublin was written by a Co. Wicklow man who is immortalised in a famous novel. He is John Francis Byrne, the friend of James Joyce. He tells the story in his autobiography, 'The Silent Years'.

Byrne was a university student in Dublin in 1902, and as his sister, two cousins and himself were in digs they decided it might be cheaper to rent a house. Towards the and of the year they heard of a vacant house on Cork Hill, about 150 yards from the entrance to the Castle Yard and almost directly opposite the City Hall. The owner was Walter Butler, Dublin City Architect.

They went along to inspect it and found it in fair condition needing minor improvements. In the top back room on the third floor they came upon a curious thing. Written in large letters over the mantlepiece was the word – 'Ghosts'. This did not worry them, and they decided to take the house, sublet the lower part as offices and use the top floor as living quarters.

While they were inspecting the house they heard footsteps in different parts of the building, but assumed they were other prospective buyers, viewing like themselves. When they came out they asked the young man from the auctioneers, who had come with the key, about the other people. To their amazement he said that no-one else had gone in.

They decided to take the house as it was, a terrific bargain, and Byrne's cousin, Mary, put down sixty pounds, a year's rent in advance. Mary got the keys and in the early afternoon went to check on repairs. While there she again heard the footsteps, especially loud on the stairs from the basement to the top. The noises were so real that she went down to the halldoor to see if it was closed. It was closed tight.

When she left she carefully checked to see if all windows were closed, then she locked the door carefully and as she did so a working man who was standing at the footpath came over and asked if he could have a word with her. He said he was a friend of her uncle's and knew her by sight. 'I want to advise you, if you're thinking of taking the house, don't do so, it's haunted,' he said.

'But,' says Mary, 'I have already taken it and got the keys.'

'Well then. ma'am, all I can say is I'm terribly sorry. It was in the basement of this very house that the Invicibles used to meet before the Phoenix Park murders. I saw them myself often and often – James Carey, young Tim Kelly, Joe Brady and the rest.'

On the next day John Byrne himself went around alone to the house with a candlestick, candles and matches. He made an investigation 'like Sherlock Holmes', but saw nothing except in the west wall of the back kitchen in the basement. In the wall was a recess bricked up which looked as if it had led into a tunnel. He left the candles etc., inside the hall-door which he locked.

That night after leaving the National Library and carrying a stout ashplant which he had cut in Carrigmore he went back to the house at about 10.15. He lit the candle, locked and bolted the door, and once more checked the house from top to bottom. Then he went up to the top floor where he decided to keep vigil.

He put out the candle, keeping the matches handy so that no-one would know the house was occupied. Some light came in from the street lamps... he heard the last tram pass by for Inchicore. At that very moment there arose from the basement a loud noise of many people tramping the kitchen floor and up the stairway into the hall. Byrne took off his overcoat, grasped his ashplant, candlestick and matches and went out on to the lobby.

The noise downstairs continued louder, then there was a thud which seemed to shake the whole house, followed by a bumping on the stairway from the hall to the basement. After a short silence heavy footsteps started to mount the first flight of stairs. Byrne lit the candle and looked down, but couldn't see anyone. The footsteps continued. He grasped his ashplant with the intention of defending himself against the intruder. The footsteps came right beside him on the lobby, and passed through the open door into the back room. He followed – there was no-one there, and the footsteps ceased.

This was the small room about thirteen feet square over the mantle piece of which was written 'Ghosts'. He checked the house again and left. The following day they decided not to take the house and they forfeited their sixty pounds.

On the night of the twenty-sixth of February, 1903, a couple of months later, one of the heaviest storms for years occured in Ireland caused untold damage. Scores of world-famed Chesterfield elms on the main road of the Phoenix Park were uprooted and destroyed. On Cork Hill the haunted house, still unlived in, stood in ruins. A chimney stack which had been blown down from the roof, had crashed down to the basement, bringing down every floor in the house with it.

Arthur Griffith's story

Mr. Robert Brennan, the former Irish Minister to Washington, told me this story which was told to him by Arthur Griffith in Gloucester Jail after the 1916 Rising.

Griffith used to travel to town every morning on the Howth tram. Very often on the same tram a fellow traveller was the late Margaret Hannigan, the well-known traditional singer, and wife of Seamus Clandillon, who was later a pioneer announcer of Radio Eireann.

Usually she was the very picture of health, but day after day she began to look worse and worse and finally Griffith asked her what was the matter. She then told him the following:

She, her husband and her children had moved into a new house in Clontarf and were only a few weeks there when she began to hear strange noises in the night which could not be attributed to mice or rats or any ordinary causes. She did not pay much attention to them.

One day, on entering her bedroom, she saw, standing in front of the dressing-table, a young lady dressed for the street. The lady turned, by-passed her without a word, and went down the stairs. The woman of the house thought that the young lady must have been a friend of the daily maid they employed, but when she questioned the maid, the latter said she had had no visitor and did not see the lady in question.

A few days later she saw the same young lady coming down the stairs. Again she passed her without a word and went on down the stairs towards the street door. Mrs. Clandillon went to the hall door and out to the front, but could see no sign of the visitor. When Seamus returned from the country on the following Saturday she told him of the strange happenings, but he only laughed at her.

During the night, however, there were a lot of noises, clearly within the house, so that they could not sleep. In the morning Seamus said that he would not sleep another night there and he appealed to her to leave it. But she was a determined character and decided to stay on.

She made some enquiries, however, and learned that the previous occupiers had left the house after only two weeks and the people before them after only three weeks. She also learned that, years earlier, the house had been occupied by a man already well on in years and his daughter, and that one day the daughter disappeared. The man told the neighbours that she had gone to some relatives in Australia and shortly afterwards he left the house himself.

Mrs. Clandillon told Arthur Griffith in the tram that she was not going to contend with the thing much longer and would get out the next day.

'When Griffith told me this tale in jail,' says Mr. Brennan, 'we agreed that when we got out we would investigate the matter, but, alas, when we got out we were both too busy and we had other things to think about. I made a note of the address of the haunted house at the time, but unfortunately I lost it afterwards.'

Haunted church

'There is a well-known Protestant church in the centre of Dublin,' writes Mr. F. W. Gumley of Glasnevin, 'which is credited with mysterious happenings from time to time and I have been able to establish two authenticated cases. The first takes us back to the twenties when one February after evening service, a curate who had scoffed at the reputed haunting remained behind to do some clerical work in the vestry.

'He directed the sexton to bolt up the main door as he had a key for the smaller entrance alongside. The sexton did as he was bidden and retired to his adjacent quarters across the churchyard. For some reason he was not quite easy in his mind having left the curate alone in the church and he returned about an hour later, going in by the smaller door already indicated. He switched on the lights and to his horror, he saw the curate lying behind the altar rails.

32

'The clergyman was in a state of coma, but soon responded to the ministrations of the alarmed sexton. He stated that having completed his work in the vestry he was about to switch off the lights when something impelled him to cross the altar. A fearful black shadow enveloped him and he fainted. He had no explanation to offer, and the matter was dropped.

'The other incident happened a couple of years ago. The assistant organist of the church in question went in one evening for his usual organ practice and ascended to the organ loft. There was a coffin covered with wreaths on the ground floor at the far end, but beyond a cursory glance the organist paid little attention.

'He was playing a hymn quietly when he heard a peculiar slithering noise from below. To his horror he saw a wreath was on the ground and even as he looked, each one of the other wreaths slid off in slow succession. He waited for no more. He jumped to his feet and was out of the church in record time. He is still not inclined to think that the reverberations of the organ caused this, as, remembering the remaining wreaths slid off when he had stopped playing. The whole affair remains a mystery.'

Mr. Gumley also tells the following story. 'A great friend of mine, a business man, and former army officer who served in various theatres of war during the 1914–1918 conflagration had supernatural experiences while living in two houses on the same road in the south Dublin suburbs. On the first occasion he was reading in bed late at night, when suddenly, feeling he was not alone, he looked up, and to his astonishment he saw the distinct form of a boy in naval uniform.

'He could make out all the details. The uniform was that of a cadet or midshipman. As he stared, the figure abruptly faded out. It did not return. He made local enquiries, and subsequently learned that a tragedy had taken place in the house. It appeared that a young midshipman home on leave with his parents was killed while sliding down the bannisters.

'On the second occasion he was preparing for bed in the stillness of the night when he heard "The swish of skirts", to quote his own words, and the rattle of the handle of his room door. He immediately associated it with the visit of his favourite aunt, opened the door but there was no-one there.

'Next morning at breakfast when he inquired if his aunt had been in the house that night he was told she had not. Later that day he learned that his aunt had died suddenly at approximately the same hour that the door handle had rattled.'

Lord Iveagh's House

Before the new regulations for Holy Week came into being there was a custom in Dublin every Holy Thursday of visiting seven churches, and offering up prayers in each, and crowds of people were seen entering and leaving each church.

When the visits were over it was not unusual for the people to go to St. Stephens's Green and stand opposite Iveagh House (now the Dept. of External Affairs) and wait to see if a cross would appear in one of the upstairs windows. If one stood in a certain place one could see what appeared to be a cross in the window concerned.

There were two versions as to why a cross was to be seen. One was that the house stood on the spot where Archbishop of Cashel was martyred in 1583, the other that many years before a servant girl in the big house who was dying was refused the consolation of seeing a priest, and when she produced a pair of rosary beads, they were thrown through the window. She died shortly afterwards, and from then on a cross was said to appear at certain times in the window.

A letter in the newspapers by a Dublin carpenter gave a different angle to the story. He said the cause was due to certain reflections inside the house, in fact, that when he went inside the house to do repairs after Lord Iveagh left, he made straight for 'the window'. He found that it was not the window of a room, but was facing a staircase and half landing.

He added: 'It was most likely that the stair bannisters and steps close to the glass were the cause of the reflections, which seemed like a cross showing on the glass. The blind was very often drawn on the window, which prevented the stairs from being seen.'

Ardee House

When the late Miss Annie M. P. Smithson, the novelist, was doing her Maternity Course she lived in the Nurses' Home at Ardee House, Ardee St., Dublin, once the Earl of Meath's Town House. It was later demolished and a hoarding now stands on the site, and the gate posts are all that remain.

'If ever a house was haunted,' she says, 'that was. One night just as I was falling asleep, I was suddenly seized and violently shaken by unseen hands. I was flung back on the pillows, trembling and terrified. I found out that this had happened to others sleeping in that room. I asked to be moved to a room upstairs — the other room had been on the ground floor — and there I slept in peace. The bathroom was another haunted place, and we all dreaded it.'

Near Finglas

'It is said that it is most unusual for two persons to see anything supernatural at the same time. Yet, this is precisely what happened to my friend and I in the neighbourhood of Finglas about twenty years ago — when this district was not the built-up area that we see to-day,' writes Mr. Jeremiah Hayes of Clontarf.

'Just coming out of our teens and, at that time, full of energy, my friend Walter and I decided, one late August afternoon, to go on a cycle tour of the Ward district west of Finglas in search of mushrooms. Having gathered a sufficient quantity of the precious fungus, we decided since the evening was overcast but warm, to explore further afield and cycle to Ashbourne.

'When leaving the village, dusk had already descended. Approaching Finglas it began to drizzle and we pushed on as quickly as possible for the city. It was just after passing Finglas village that the incident hap-

36

pened. We were both cycling abreast when we simultaneously noticed a weird figure keeping up with us on the footpath.

'Although bewildered, and in my case, a bit frightened, we braked hard and dismounted. We looked at each other to make sure that we were not seeing things and again looked at the figure. It was no illusion! There he was in glowing outline looking at us – a tall, thin, middle aged man, clean shaven and wearing a peaked cap – drifting along on the footpath and, through him, we could clearly discern the stones of an old stone wall adjoining the path.

'Upon reaching an opening in the wall where a laneway meets the road, the apparition, accompanied by a noise similar to air rushing into a vacuum, turned into the laneway and disappeared, as the hissing sound changed to that of a melancholy moan. (Incidentally, the old wall where this incident happened is still there, also the laneway – a housing estate now occupies portion of the land once bordered by the wall.)

'Needless to remark, we mounted our bicycles quickly and, barely speaking a word, made our way to our respective abodes. Taking into consideration the fact that it was very misty and drizzling obliterates any chance of shadows being cast and our imagination then playing tricks with us. My friend, Walter, was killed in a tragic accident on the continent a few year later.'

CHAPTER 4

The Banshee and other death warnings

The Banshee

'Not for low-born English hucksters, waileth our banshee,' wrote James Clarence Mangan, referring to the fact that only the purest blooded Irish families were followed by this strange lady. As Mike McInerney says in Lady Gregory's 'The Workhouse Ward' — 'she only screeched for the five families... the Hyneses, the Foxes, the Faheys, the Dooleys, the McInerneys.' He was of course only referring to his own area of the West.

The origin of the banshee is rather obscure. The original *sidhe bhean* (woman of the fairy) was a beautiful maiden from *Tir-na-nOg* (Land of Youth), and such a one was Niamh of the Golden Hair who carried Oisin away with her. Perhaps it was years of persecution by Danes and English that turned the banshee into a withered screeching hag, combing her tousled hair with a broken comb.

Up to the beginning of this century stories of the banshee were legion. Elliott O'Donnell the famous ghost story collector tells of one who appeared in an old house, 'not five minutes from St. Stephen's Green, Dublin' in 'The McGrath Banshee'. She had 'very blue eyes and a kind of reddish-gold hair that was not screwed up on her head, but hanging in curls on her shoulders, and wearing a bright green dress.' She appears to a little boy who later dies.

The most famous banshee was Aibhill, who followed the Royal house of the O'Briens and who appeared on the rock of Craglea, above Killaloe, near the old palace of Kincora. Before the aged Brian Boru set off to fight the Danes in the Battle of Clontarf in A.D. 1014 he knew he would never return alive, for the previous night Aibhill was said to have appeared to him to tell him of his impending fate.

The late Miss Annie Smithson, the popular Irish novelist, tells in her autobiography how while nursing in Co. Clare about 50 years ago she had some strange experiences. One night her companion and herself were awakened by a most awful sound:

'It was like the long drawn-out wailing of a soul in torment. The Banshee, I thought, and began to feel that horrid prickling of the scalp which we describe by saying that "our hair rose". On and on it went, wailing back and forth among the rocks in a wild bit of woodland, just across the road from our cottage. A lost soul in torment – the cry of one lost forever – forever wandering in the outer darkness. Near morning the wailing stopped, and we fell asleep.'

'Later that day one of my patients said to me: "So the Banshee was on the rocks last night – were ye frightened?" I heard nothing about any death in the area but I shall never forget that wailing.'

'I remember my father, whose name was Byrne, often telling me how the Banshee followed the Byrne family, and he told me the following incidents of his own experiences. His home and place of birth was in County Armagh, near the foot of Slieve Gullion, writes Mrs. K. Callery of Kilkenny.

'He was standing outside his own door on a bright moonlit night about eleven p.m. and looking across to his cousin's house, which lay beyond a few fields, he noticed a light there, and thought something must be amiss in it, as the family usually retired early. He stood there wondering if he should go over, in case they required any help, as there was only his aged uncle and aunt and their three daughters, one of whom had been unwell for years.

'Then he heard a long wailing cry. The cry seemed to go round and round one of the fields between his house and the house of his cousins. Still he stood there, not daring to move while the wailing continued. He said afterwards that it was a long, heartbreaking cry which went on all through the night.

'Surely,' he thought, ''tis the banshee: some of the Byrnes, or the Haggarts, or the Hanaways, must be going to die, as they are all connections of the Byrnes and that for certain is the Banshee.' Next morning a messenger brought the sad news to his house that his cousin Mary, the delicate girl, had died early that morning.

'There were other similar incidents relating to the Banshee which he often told to me, and certainly from his sincere revelations it could not have been imagination.'

Over fifty years ago reports of a banshee terrified residents in the Sandyford area of Co. Dublin, and in this connection I have the following tale from my friend Denis Brennan, the actor and well-known radio personality: 'I was born and spent most of my boyhood in the village of Sandyford, and I heard a lot of local lore from my mother and my late grandmother. This incident came from my grandmother to my mother, and so to me.

My grandmother, a Mrs. Haydon (who will be well remembered by the older inhabitants) knew a family by the name of Pielow who owned a quite extensive farm across the road from her house. The portion of this farm near the house known as "the haggard" where the hay was stored when drawn in, was, reputedly, a great haunt of our "Sandyford Banshee". My grandmother reported many a sleepless night as a result of her caterwauling.

'Mr. Pielow was a practical man. Such disturbances were not to be tolerated! One night, having been awakened from his peaceful slumbers by this howling, the good gentleman lost his temper. He went to the stable, took down a large horsewhip, marched to "the haggard", dressed in pants pulled up about his nightshirt, and on being confronted by "the Banshee", proceeded to attempt to belabour her with the whip.

'After the first stroke, the "Banshee" screamed loudly, and flung a comb, with which she had been combing her hair, at him. He staggered back, but succeeded in whipping the little woman out of the haggard. Then feeling quite satisfied that he had rid himself of a human nuisance he returned to his bed. He never left it again alive! He took ill that night, and died soon after.'

Only last year weird wailings were heard in the seaside town of Youghal which the local people took to be a banshee. The wailings were heard all over the town, not every night, they were not heard perhaps for a few nights and then started all over again. For many nights young men, armed with torches scoured the area but the cause remained a mystery.

It is easy to imagine that fifty years ago, before the many distractions and noises of our modern age, a person hearing the screech of an owl or the cry of a cat in the dead stillness of the night would imagine it to be the banshee. Indeed, over thirty years ago there was consternation in Coolock, Co. Dublin when residents heard each night the wailings of what they thought was the banshee. It later turned out to be a dying golden owl in a barn.

Its frequent nightly appearances with wings outspread and its terrifying cries put fear into the hearts of people homeward bound.

Knocks on door

There is a strong tradition in many parts of Ireland that some families are warned of the approaching death of one of their members by three knocks on the door. My late grandmother, God rest her, believed that it followed our family and claimed she always heard the knocks about midnight when a death had occurred. Many a night, as a child, I trembled when I heard a knock on the door as I lay awake in bed on a winter's night.

In Seymour and Neligan's 'True Irish Ghost Stories' a Mrs. Acheson of Co. Roscommon tells of a mysterious knocking. She wrote: 'Emo House, Co. Westmeath, a very old mansion since pulled down, was purchased by my grandfather for his son, my father. The latter had only been living in it for a few days when knocking commenced at the hall door. Naturally he thought it was someone playing tricks, or endeavouring to frighten him away.

'One night he had the lobby window open directly over the door. The knocking commenced, and he looked out: it was a very bright night, and as there was no porch he could see the door distinctly; the knocking continued, but he did not see the knocker move. Another night he sat up expecting his brother, but as the latter did not come he went to bed. Finally the knocking went on so consistently that he felt sure his brother had arrived.

'He went downstairs and opened the door but no one was there. Still convinced that his brother was there and had gone round to the yard to put up his horse, he went out; but scorcely had he gone twenty yards from the door when the knocking recommenced behind his back. On turning round he could see no one.

'Eventually the knocking got so bad that he could not rest. But he had not mentioned the strange occurrence to any one. One morning he went up through the fields between four and five a.m. To his surprise he found the herd out feeding the cattle. My father asked him why he was out so early. He replied that he could not sleep.

' "Why?" asked my father. "You know why yourself, sir – the knocking." He then found that this man had heard it all the time, though he slept at the end of a long house. My father was advised to take no notice of it for it would go as it came, though at this time it was continuous and very loud, and so it did. The country people said it was the late resident who could not rest.

'We had another curious and most eerie experience in this house. A former rector was staying the night with us, and as the evening wore on we began to tell ghost stories. He related some remarkable experiences, and as we were talking the drawing-room door suddenly opened as wide as possible, and then slowly closed again. It was a calm night, and at any rate it was a heavy double door which never flies open however strong the wind may be blowing.

'Everyone in the house was in bed, as it was after midnight, except the three persons who witnessed this namely myself, my daughter and the rector. The effect on the latter was most marked. He was a big, strong, jovial man and a good athlete, but when he saw the door open he quivered like an aspen leaf.'

Globe of light

An unusual tale is told by Mrs. V. Smyth of Roundwood, Co. Wicklow. 'One night during World War Two I went to bed about ten o'clock. I read a book for some time, and then, after putting out the light, composed myself for sleep. I must have dozed off, for suddenly I was awakened by a dull thud in the kitchen, a sound like a sack of wet sand or clay falling from the roof to the floor.

'I sat up, and glancing towards my bedroom door, saw a luminous globe of light floating in the doorway. On that minute my blood froze and I was unable to move. I shut my eyes, and on opening them again, the globe of light had vanished, and power had returned to my body.

'When I lit the light everything was as usual, and there was nothing to account for the noise which had awakened me. But during the week the news came that a cousin of mine had been lost at sea. The ship in which he had been serving had been torpedoed that night. That was only one of the many death warnings I have received.'

Scanlan lights

Another strange death warning was the 'Scanlan lights', said to be connected with the Scanlan family of Bally-knockane, Co. Limerick, and seen frequently on the death of a member. The origin of the lights is connected with a well-known Irish legend.

Scanlan Mor (who died in 640 A.D.), King of Ossory, from whom the family claim descent was placed in prison by the High King, Aedh Ainmire. When St. Colmcille attended the Synod of Drom Ceat he pleaded with Aedh to free his captive, but the High King refused, whereupon the saint said that Scanlan Mor would be free that night and would unloose his (the saint's) shoes.

Colmcille left the gathering, and that night a bright pillar of fire appeared in the air, and hung over the hut where Scanlan was imprisoned. A beam of light darted into the room where he lay, and a voice called to him, telling him to shake off his fetters. In amazement he did so, and was led past his guards by an angel to the place where Colmcille was staying, just as the saint was about to unloose his shoes for the night. Scanlan, in gratitude, insisted on unloosing them himself just as the saint had prophesied. Seymour and Neligan reported that the lights appeared in 1913 when a member of the family died.

The Gormanston foxes

The crest of the Viscounts Gormanston is a running fox, while the animal forms one of the supporters of the family's Coat-of-Arms. One of the strangest stories imaginable is told about this family, the Prestons.

They resided in their family seat, Gormanston Castle, Co. Meath. If the head of the house died the foxes from the surrounding countryside used leave the coverts and congregate at the castle. This happened when Jenico, the Twelfth Viscount lay dying in 1860; the foxes were seen about and moving towards the house for some days previously. Just before his death three foxes were playing about and making noise close to the house, just in front of 'the Cloisters' (yew trees planted and trained in that shape).

The foxes came in pairs into the demesne and sat under the Viscount's window, and barked and howled all night. Next morning they were found all around the house. They walked through the poultry without touching them, nor were they themselves touched by the dogs. After the funeral they returned to their natural habitat, and the laws of nature resumed their course.

The same occurences marked the deaths in 1876 of Edward, the thirteenth Viscount; in 1907 of Jenico, the fourteenth Viscount and in 1925 of Jenico Edward the fifteenth Viscount. Jenico William the sixteenth Viscount was said to be missing and believed killed after the fall of France in 1940. But as no foxes were seen around the castle, the local people were of the opinion that he was still alive.

Gormanston Castle has since been taken over by the Franciscan Fathers and is now Luke Wadding College, so that if any foxes were seen walking tamely around nowadays the reason might be that they know that the place is under the patronage of the followers of the saint who loved animals and called them his brothers.

The Preston family came to Ireland from Lancashire early in the fourteenth century and settled as merchants in Drogheda. They acquired the Gormanston property in 1363 when Sir Roger de Preston acquired it from Almarious de Saint Amand. The tittle, Viscount of Gormanston, was created in 1478.

A local resident gave the following as the reason for appearance of the foxes; In the seventeenth century one of the Viscounts Gormanston was taking part in a hunt when the fox was located in a secluded part of the demesne. The hounds were going in for 'the kill' when the Viscount saw the fox was a vixen and was trying to protect her litter from the dogs. He had the pack called off and just before his death the foxes made their first appearance around the castle.

A colleague of mine heard another interesting story from an old woman who lived near the castle. When Cromwell was on his way to Drogheda to carry out one of the most barbaric massacres in history, the then Viscount was not in the castle but his lady and young son and heir, a child only a few years old, were. The family had a pet baboon, and the butler seeing the merciless Roundheads in the distance had an idea. He gave the child to the baboon who immediately took it in his arms and climbed with it to an inaccessible part of the battlements.

When Cromwell and his officers arrived, he was received by Lady Gormanston. 'Whose castle is this?' growled the Lord Protector as she opened the main door. The quick-witted lady replied: 'Gormanston's today, Cromwell's tomorrow.' The tyrant was so intrigued by the reply that for once he refrained from sacking and burning the castle. He and his officers stayed the night there, and continued on to Drogheda the next day, oblivious of the fact that the heir was safe and sound in the care of the baboon from whom he was taken when the soldiers had gone.

There is a group of trees at the back of the castle still known as Cromwell's copse. There is a large standing stone in front of the moat which for some strange reason is called 'Cromwell's Granny'.

CHAPTER 5

Poltergeists

There have been many cases of poltergeists recorded in Ireland. A poltergeist is a noisy, sprightly spirit, who in nearly all cases remains invisible. It manifests its presence by banging on doors or hammering, and throwing objects around, sometimes very heavy ones. Rarely, however does it injure anyone.

These visitants seem to be attracted to houses where there are young children, and in many cases where a young girl has just reached puberty.

There was a case in 1877 at the lonely village of Derrygonnelly, nine miles from Enniskellen in the home of a farmer who had been left a widower with a family of four girls and a boy. The eldest child, Margaret, aged about twenty seemed to be the centre of the disturbance. Strange rappings and scratchings were at first heard; then objects began to move around, stones began to fall, and candles and boots were repeatedly thrown out of the window.

The family, who were Methodists, placed an open Bible on the bed with a big stone on top of it. Some unseen power, however, displaced the Bible, and eventually removed it from the room tearing several pages from it. Candles and lamps mysteriously disappeared.

Sir William Barrett F.R.S., a well-known investigator of psychical phenomena at the time, visited the farmhouse. He heard long continued knockings some of which were like 'those made by a carpenter's hammer driving nails into floorings'. He was satisfied that the noise could not have been made by anyone in the house. He saw stones fall from nowhere. The Professor challenged the mysterious agent to answer questions by knocks. When he mentally thought of numbers the raps indicated the correct ones.

In Enniscorthy

In Enniscorthy in July 1910 a more lively intruder disturbed a family. Apart from hammering and other noises in this case, the poltergeist's favourite trick was to pull all the bed clothes off a bed and then move the heavy bedstead from one part of the room to the other. Three young men slept in the room, all of whom were reduced to a state of abject terror.

The principal sufferer was a youth of eighteen named Randall. On one occasion, investigators in the room saw sheets and blankets pulled off him and he himself dragged out of bed on to the floor. A chair danced by itself in the middle of the room, and when the three terrified young men got into the one bed together the bed turned on its side pitching them on to the floor.

In County Down

Two others cases of poltergeists were recorded in Co. Down. In the residence of a farmer, Peter McCrory of Lenagh, near Mountfield in 1865 turf clods were thrown by an invisible source all over the kitchen, terrifying the family. A incredulous neighbour who called in was unwise enough to say 'why don't they clod me?' No sooner were the words out of his mouth when three stones struck him in the back whereupon he promptly took to his heels!

In November, 1876 in the house of Mr. Allen of Cookstown the intruder broke windows over a period of months, and although a careful watch was kept no-one could see how it was done. Some panes were broken with stones, and others seemed to break by themselves. Bowls shot off the table and smashed; coats and hats disappeared from pegs; potatoes jumped out of pots into the fire, and stones weighing three pounds or more hopped down the stairs.

Eerie assignment

Mr. P. J. Donaghy, a well-known journalist tells how as a young reporter he was sent on an eerie assignment in 1934 to the North of Ireland. There had been reports of extraordinary activities in the home of a small farmer near Articlave village, on the Coleraine-Castlerock road. A poltergeist was said to be making life unbearable for the farmer, his wife and a family of two sons and a daughter. Articles moved around the house of their own accord; and delph, clothes and lamp globes were flung about under the eyes of the family.

The daughter, a little girl of ten was said to be the centre of the disturbances. While in bed at night she was troubled by ghostly knockings, and by sharp instruments like needles being stuck into her. Now over to Mr. Donaghy:

'The storm was rising when I found the house on a desolate bit of land off the main road. It was an ordinary two-story country house, owned by a Presbyterian family. About twenty neighbours were in the kitchen when I went in, and I was welcomed by the father and made to sit at the big peat fire where I was to spend most of the night and morning. After these disturbances began, neighbours remained with the family most of the night and I was not surprised at the number of people in the house. The kitchen was lighted by a single oil lamp placed in the middle of the table.

'The daughter was there – a shy, intelligent country child, who looked and acted like any other girl of her age. I was impressed by the demeanour of the people present. If all these happenings had an origin in practical joking, these were not the type of people to be involved, and certainly not to carry it to the stage it had reached.

'Before midnight a car was heard outside the house, and three people who might be described as "substantial" people of the district, arrived to take up their vigil in the house.

'After midnight the neighbours began to leave, and before one o'clock the only people in the house were the members of the family, the three vigil keepers and myself. I sat at the fire with the two sons of the house, and occasionally the three visitors. As the hours passed, conversation waned. The wind was really howling outside now, it sighed in the chimney and the rain beat on the kitchen windows. A collie dog lay asleep beside the hearth, his head on his outstretched paws. Now and again the dog raised his ears and his head, listened, and a whimper or a growl rose in his throat. It was probably the storm. Shortly after five a.m. we were shaken by a whisper from the staircase. Something was happening in Laura's room.

'We filed up the stairs and into the room. It was about ten feet square, the child lay on a bed alongside the wall which was the outside wall of the house, and the only window in the room was over the bed. The room was lit by two candles, and Laura's mother sat on the top of the bed. Laura was sitting upright in the bed, and for some moments I could distinguish nothing unusual or alarming.

'Then I began to hear the knocking. It was a clear tap-tapping like the sound made by a knuckle rapped sharply on a piece of wood. It seemed to be coming from the wall, the outside stone wall of the house, near the bottom of the child's bed. We all sat there listening intently to the tapping, and I tried to identify the sound. It came regularly in single or double taps.

'It was always distinct, sometimes rising to an alarming volume, and occasionally there was a series of fast, confused, impatient tapping.

'I don't think there is any explanation which has been suggested to me or which occurred to me then or since that I did not test in that room that night, using at times an electric torch, until the courtesy and the patience of the people there became clearly strained. But the tapping baffled me.

'Although by putting my ear close to the wall I

could almost pin-point the spot from which it was coming (about two feet above the floor), my hand placed on the wall could find no vibration. The queer thing about it was that I could not place exactly the point from which the tapping was coming – it seemed to move around in an elusive, maddening way.

'A tree branch tapping on the outside wall in the storm? I pulled down the window and looked out. No tree – nothing.

'For more than two hours after this I was present at a scene I will never forget. For all that time I listened as one of those present, a prominent man in the community, chanted off questions to Something that tapped back the answers. By the code system of "yes" or "no" used on an elimination basis the strange tapping answered at least a hundred questions – all of them correctly. For instance the month, the date of the month, and the year of my birth – correctly.

'Scores of such intimate questions, the answers to which were completely unknown to anyone else in the room, were answered about all of us. Some time, still very early in the morning, the sound in the room stopped altogether, and after a long period of silence I decided to take my leave.

'I have discussed this experience with many people since and read a great del more about such happenings. Now, years later, my verdict remains the same – *unexplained.*'

Dublin Castle

A coal-shovelling poltergeist who switched off the
light persecuted gardai in Dublin Castle, according to
an article in the Garda Review in November, 1955,
written by Sergeant Lowe. When he had completed his
training, Sergeant (then Garda) Lowe was given sleeping quarters in the castle. Fourteen men slept in the
room.

One night he was in bed alone all the other men were
on duty, when someone switched off the light. He
thought some of the others were playing a joke, and
jumped out of bed and switched on the light again. He
opened the door, but there was nobody there. He got
back into bed and the same thing happened. Then he
heard someone shovelling coal into the kitchen range.
The range had only the capacity for three shovelfulls,
but the shovelling went on and on.

Garda Lowe got out of bed and crept down the passage towards the kitchens. The shovelling continued.
He slowly opened the door and quickly switched on
the kitchen light. The shovelling stopped abruptly.
There was no-one in the room, and the fire was nearly
out. Nothing had been put on the range for hours and
the shovel stood in its usual position against the wall.

Near Croom

A series of unusual incidents in and around a four-
roomed cottage at Honeypound, near Croom, Co.
Limerick, occupied by a brother and sister hit the head-

lines in August, 1957. The cottage was occupied by a retired nurse, Mrs. Margaret O'Callaghan and her brother, Mr. John Broughton.

At first flowers planted around the cottage were up-rooted and thrown about the door. When replanted they were again uprooted. Then things moved about inside the house. Pictures were taken from the wall and flung on the floor. Bread disappeared from the table, later to appear under chair cushions and in odd places. Towels, soap and eggs were thrown into the milk and water.

The keys of the doors were taken away. Bedroom doors which had been locked at night, were found open in the morning. Most of these happenings took place around noon. The poltergeist, if such it was, ceased its activities after the local clergy had blessed the house, and a Mass had been offered.

CHAPTER 6

Haunted castles

Castlegarde, County Limerick

A twelfth century castle tower near Pallasgreen, Co. Limerick, is haunted by a ghost which glides up and down the winding stone staircase in a gown of rustling silk. The story of 'The Lady in Silk' was told to Mr. Liam Shine by Mrs. Sybil Thompson, wife of Mr. Hugh Edward Thompson, who inherited the castle named Castlegarde from his uncle, Lord Gilliemore.

Here is the story as it appeared in the Evening Herald in January, 1955:

'"I was sleeping in the third floor bedroom in the tower at the time," said Mrs. Thompson. "I was awakened at about one o'clock to hear a sound like the swish of silk on the stair-case. The rustling continued for a time as if the person was moving up the stairs. Then it stopped and though I lay awake all night I heard nothing else. I heard no footsteps, nothing except the rustle of silk."

'There was no explanation for the noise except the story of the ghost that haunts the tower. The bedroom in which Mrs. Thompson slept that night is no longer occupied. No one knows the full story of the ghostly lady in silk but legend links her with victims of the "murder hole" in the tower.

'Mrs. Thompson pointed out the "murder hole" which once had a door on the third floor like other bedrooms in the tower. The door led to a man-made chasm between the thick outer wall of the tower and another wall built a few feet inside it. The unsuspecting guest who stepped through the doorway fell fifty feet to the bottom of the murder hole.

'A bedroom at the top of the .seventy-foot high tower is also vacant. "No one would sleep in either bedroom," said Mrs. Thompson, "but the bedrooms in the lower floors of the tower are occupied. The lady in silk seems to stick to the upper floors."

'Mrs. Thompson said she once went to the top storey room on a perfectly calm night. Just as she was leaving the room a strong gust of wind came out of nowhere and blew out the oil lamp she was carrying. She said she had never been in the room at night since. She believed the tower was haunted and that the rustling silk came from a ghost.

'Mr. Thompson said: "I don't believe in ghosts and I think there is some other explanation, but there is certainly a legend that the tower is haunted and we could never explain the sound of rustling silk heard by my wife. I once slept alone in the house and I saw or heard no ghosts though I don't mind admitting it was very lonely and a bit creepy."

'Mr. Thompson went on to say that there was only one historical record of a murder at Castlegarde. It was told of an Elizabethan General who swooped on the castle and cut off the head of the aged owner.

'He also said: "The tower was built in 1198 and is probably the oldest inhabited house in Ireland. An extension was built a few hundred years ago with a head of Brian Boru carved in stone over the main entrance.

58

There is a tradition that there was a four-mile long underground passage to another stronghold of the O'Grady's at Toher which is now in ruins." '

Luttrellstown

A colleague of mine, who wishes to remain anonymous, told me the following story: Lord Luttrell fought on the side of King James in the Battle of the Boyne, but when he saw the tide was turning against James he changed over with his men to King William, and so saved his estates from forfeiture. Some years afterwards he was being carried down Stafford Street (now Wolfe Tone Street) in a sedan chair when a dandy who was walking nearby drew his sword and plunged it into the noble Lord's heart.

Luttrell was buried in the castle in North Co. Dublin that bears his name but some time afterwards some of his enemies dug up his bones and scattered them all over the place. Some years ago, my friend had to call to the castle on business. It was a dark winter's evening, and when he was leaving he had to walk down the long avenue to the gates.

'After I had walked about a hundred yards,' he says, 'suddenly I heard footsteps behind me. I looked back and saw a white figure following me. I stopped and the figure stopped also. When I continued the figure did likewise and kept in step with me. When I crossed the little bridge the figure followed but it did not come any further. I could still see it as I hurried towards the gate and I felt positive I had seen the ghost of Lord Luttrell.'

Thousands of visitors who pass through Carrickfergus Castle each year are shown 'Buttoncap's Well' which is said to be called after a ghost which haunts the castle. The story goes as follows: a native of the town, one Robert Rainey joined a regiment stationed in the castle. He was reputed to be of a wayward nature and became the companion of a fellow soldier, Tim Lavery, a drummer in the regimental band. The men were of the same age, size, and dressed alike.

Rainey often went to Whiteabbey to court a girl by the name of Betsy Baird who had promised to marry him. One night after kissing her goodbye Rainey was about to trudge back to Carrickfergus when he heard footsteps coming across the road. Taking cover he noticed it was the brother of the colonel of his regiment, a Captain Jennings, who had also been making love to Betsy, unknown to Rainey.

In a death bed confession years afterwards Rainey said: 'Hell's fire raged in my bosom, and in my fierceness of wrath against my rival, worthy only of a fiend, I flew after him and ran my sword twice through his body. The captain yelled "Lavery, you have murdered me." I didn't want to hear any more, so I rushed to the sea, washed the weapon, and hurried back to my quarters and to bed.

Lavery was of course arrested on the mistaken thought of the dying captain, and hanged for a crime he did not commit. Before the sentence was carried out he said: 'When I get to the other world I'll be revenged on you all. I'll haunt the castle and none of you will have any rest.'

Lavery had been known among the soldiers by the nickname, 'Buttoncap' because he wore a large button in the centre of his cockade, so that when his ghost was seen in later years it was known as 'Buttoncap's Ghost'.

Killarney

The ghost of the O'Donaghue of the Glens, is said to be seen on a white horse, accompanied by a host of friends, relatives and retainers, riding around the lakes of Killarney. They were said to ride around the lakes every May-Day Eve to the sound of ghostly music. Years ago many people reported that while standing on the lake shores they heard enchanting music coming up from the depths. The ruins of Ross Castle, the O'Donaghue's family seat, and the old Weir Bridge are both said to be haunted.

Kilgobbin

Kilgobbin Castle, near Stepaside, Co. Dublin is said to be haunted by the ghost of a woman in chains but I have never been able to get any details about this legend. The castle originally belonged to the Walsh family from whom it passed, by forfeiture or otherwise in the reign of Charles I, into the possession of Sir Adam Loftus of Rathfarnham.

In Gola Castle, near the village of Scotstown, Co. Monaghan several people claim to have seen a strange green light, which appears at certain times. Some local people who went to investigate were walking down the stone stairway when the light suddenly appeared to be coming after them. They got frigthened and ran, but it brushed past them, and they said it felt like a cold breeze. At the same time there was a heavy noise like a rattle of thunder echoing all through the castle.

CHAPTER 7

The Hungry Grass

The publication recently of 'The Great Hunger' by Mrs. Cecil Woodham-Smith has recalled one of the most tragic episodes in our history, and one that was bitterly remembered for generations afterwards. It was from this period that the legend of 'the hungry grass' evolved. This tale has been related in many parts of the country, and was featured in many novels, particularly those of James Murphy.

In comparatively recent years that Grand Old Man of the Dublin hills, Malachy Horan told Dr. Little about such an adventure:

'One day, many years ago, I got word to cross the mountain for a chance of buying some yearling ewes. I had not long set out before I fell in with two neighbour-men, and glad enough I was of their company. It is mortal lonesome up in those hills. They are so full of the old ancient things.

'There is the Kenny's Stone, Killenarden graveyard where the old kings lie buried, St. Moling's Well in Toomaling that cures the bad stomachs, the Rath at Ballinascorney and a mart of other things. There is something about those places that makes a man glad of company and gladder still when he is past them.

'Well, it did not take us long to reach Sally Gap, what with talking and the fine day that was there. We took the short cuts along the sheep paths through the furze. I was in great heart – never felt better in my life. Suddenly, without a moment's warning, a terrible feeling took hold of me. My stomach fell in as if with the most awful hunger, my knees trembled and the sight left my eyes. A sweat, so cold that it froze my blood, broke out on me.

'I fell on my hands and knees and knew that I would die in a few minutes. One of the men I was with looked back and saw how things were with me. He came to me and reaching into his pocket, took out a morsel of bread which he forced into my mouth and... in less time than it takes to tell the life came back into my body.'

Malachy's companion told him never to cross the hills again without a piece of bread in his pocket. He described the grass as white and herb-like. 'Like keeb it lies lank in Autumn and mostly grows by the sheep-walks.'

The late Annie M. P. Smithson, tells in her autobiography of an experience she had as a district nurse in Clare. She was on her way to a maternity case when she walked on the 'hungry grass'. She managed to stumble into her patient's cottage and gasped out the word, 'bread'. The old grandmother cut a slice off a loaf and handed it to her with a glass of milk.

'Did you come by the Cross Roads?' and then, she asked, 'you came upon the hungry grass.' 'The doctor there told me,' writes Miss Smithson, 'that he had had a similar experience. The people say that these patches of grass on the roadside are where the victims of the Famine lay down to die.'

Another strange belief is that of the *'foidin mear-aidhe* (stray sod). This tells of an unfortunate nocturnal traveller who walks upon a certain patch of ground, and has to keep walking in circles, so to speak, until the moon rises. The only alternative, so they say, is to turn one's coat inside out and the spell is broken. I knew one hard-boiled journalist who confessed to me that he had done so on one occasion.

Another acquaintance of mine claims that he was lost once in a haunted glen in a wild part of Co. Wicklow, and that he was absolutely terrified before he finally was able to escape from it!

Black dog

In many parts of Ireland there are stories of the appearance of a Black Dog usually believed to be the devil in disguise. When I was a boy living in Rialto in Dublin an old man told me a blood-curdling tale of an encounter he had with a Black dog one dark winter's night as he walked along the banks of the Grand Canal between Rialto Bridge and Inchicore Bridge fifty years before.

He said it approached from the darkness and confronted him with blazing eyes. When he made the Sign of the Cross it leaped into the air and disappeared into the waters of the canal without making a sound. For years after I heard this tale whenever I encountered any dog in the darkness my hair almost began to stand on end. Since then I have heard many stories of Black Dogs being seen in all parts of the country.

A variation of the story is that of a strange dog which comes to the doorway of a house and stays in the house for days or weeks and then just as mysteriously disappears.

Devil's horse

Many tales have been handed down from father to son and one of these is the one about the blacksmith 'who shoed the devil's horse'. A knock at the door late at night: the blacksmith is called from his bed by a dark stranger in a hurry. The stranger says he will pay well so the smith reluctantly agrees to do the job.

When the horse is shod the stranger thrusts a golden guinea into the smith's hand, and jumps on his horse and rides off. To his horror the smith notices the rider has cloven feet. Then looking at the money in his hand he finds it is just a piece of glass.

In parts of Co. Kerry there is a belief that if a tombstone is not erected over the grave of the dead before the year of the death is out, his next of kin will die. This has given rise to many ghost stories of spirits being seen.

CHAPTER 8

From Kerry to Belfast

Room in Maynooth

Many people have heard of the haunted room in
Maynooth College, which is situated in the junior divi-
sion in Rhetoric House. The room was originally Room
No. two on the top corridor. It is now an oratory of
St. Joseph. There are many versions of the haunting
but here is what Father Denis Meehan says in his excellent book, 'Window on Maynooth':

'The incident, whatever it may have been, is at least
dated to some extent by a Trustee's resolution of Oc-
tober 23, 1860 – "that the President be authorised to
convert room No. 2 on the top corridor of Rhetoric
House into an Oratory of St. Joseph, and to fit up an
oratory of St. Aloysius in the prayer hall of the Junior
Students."

'The story, as it is commonly now retailed, for the
edification of susceptible Freshmen, begins with a
suicide. The student resident in this room killed himself
one night. According to some he used a razor; but
tellers are not too careful about such details. The next
inhabitant, it is alleged, felt irresistibly impelled to fol-
low suit, and again, according to some, he did. A third,
or it may have been the second, to avoid a similar im-
pulse, and when actually about to use his razor, jumped
through the window into Rhetoric yard. He broke
some bones, but saved his life.

'Subsequently, no student could be induced to use the room; but a priest volunteered to sleep or keep vigil there for one night. In the morning his hair was white, though no one dares to relate what his harrowing experiences may have been. Afterwards the front wall of the room was removed and a small altar of St. Joseph was erected.

'The basic details of the story have doubtless some foundation in fact, and it is safe to assume that something very unpleasant did occur. The suicide (or suicides), in so far as one can deduce from the oral traditions that remain seem to have taken place in the period 1842–48. A few colourful adjuncts, that used to form part of the stock in trade of the story teller, are passing out of memory now. Modern students, for instance, do not point out the footprint burned into the wood, or the bloodmarks on the walls.'

Killed by steam tram

Malachy Horan told Dr. George A. Little about an unusual ghost. Here it is as related in 'Malachy Horan Remembers':

'I remember 40 years ago a poor man was killed by the Blessington steam tram between Jobstown and Templeogue... soon afterwards I was at the January fair at Naas. I stopped at Carroll's Inn there till after 11 o'clock. Then I started for home.

'At a part of the Saggart Road that is overhung by trees, a man's shoulder struck mine. I wished him "good night" but he did not answer. Confounding him under my breath, I started a bit of a song. A few yards further and I was struck again.

' "Can't you mind where you are going," I asked, real angry. I get no answer. It happened again, and this time I did not speak... a cold sweat broke out on my head and in the small of my back. I tried to think what to do. It was as long to go on as to go back. Every now and then the thing bumped me... I knew it was no living man.'

Eventually Malachy reached a neighbour's cottage. He hammered at the door with his stick. The neighbour opened the door. 'I saw his jaw drop and his eyes stare. I looked behind for the first time. The hair pushed my old hat off my head. A fully dressed man stood behind me, but he had no head!'

The two men rushed into the cottage and barred the door, and said a prayer. 'We said a prayer for his soul,' Malachy added. 'It was never seen after. Maybe the prayers found him rest.'

Loftus Hall

Loftus Hall in County Wexford, on the east bank of the Suir, was built on the site of a stronghold erected by Raymond, one of Strongbow's followers. His descendants forfeited it in 1641 after the ill-fated insurrection, and the property subsequently fell into the hands of the Loftus family, one of whom built the house and other buildings. About the middle of the eighteenth century there lived at the Hall, Charles Tottenham, a member of the Irish Parliament, who was known as 'Tottenham of the Boots', because he had made an historic ride to Dublin to give his casting vote in a motion which saved the Irish Treasury £80,000.

It was Tottenham's custom to invite a number of his aristocratic friends to convene there in the autumn for shooting parties. A member of one of those parties happened to be a handsome young nobleman with whom his daughter fell in love.

For some reason or other the father strongly objected to the affair and refused to give his permission for her to wed. This had the effect of turning her from a vivacious light-hearted girl to one of a very moody and despondent dispostion. She pined away and died. Her ghost was seen in that house for years afterwards.

One night a long time after the tragedy, the father had a shooting party in the house and one man stayed up late cleaning his gun for the following day's sport. About midnight the door of the room opened and in walked a lovely young girl dressed in white.

The apparition was so sudden and unexpected that he dropped the gun in fright. She walked across the room and disappeared at the far end. The parish priest, Father Broaders, was appealed to and he exorcised the ghost.

In the old cemetery in Horetown there is a tombstone with a verse which ends:

> And Father Broaders the best of all,
> Who banished the ghost from Loftus Hall.

Mr. S. Stevenson of Belfast had a strange experience in Co. Antrim in 1951. He set off with his wife on a camping holiday from Glengormley, heading for the back of Cavehill by way of Hightown Road, and leading on to the Horseshoe Road. 'We had decided to pitch our tent up on the side of the hill but all of a sudden the weather changed and we retired into an old tumbled-down house, with the permission of the owner, a farmer, who lived about a mile away.

'Now this house had only one good part, a room, which apart from broken windows was in good shape, and at least it sheltered us from the rain. After we had bedded down for the night at about 11.30, I heard the noise of a horse and van, and a man's voice shouting "Get up there", as the horse galloped past outside. Now as the farmer had told us that some gipsies were camped nearby I did not pay much attention to the happening.

'The next night, however, the same thing happened at exactly the same time. I did not say anything to my wife at the time in case it would frighten her, but I decided that if it happened the next night, I would go out and investigate. Sure enough, on the third night at the same time I heard the same noise of the clip-clop of the horse, the wheels of the van on the road and the shouting of the man.

'I rushed out, but although I could still hear the sounds I could see nothing, although the night was clear. Later I mentioned it to the farmer, who said he had never experienced anything himself but that an old gipsy had died in the house years before so perhaps it was his ghost I heard.'

Poet Returned

A strong friendship existed between the poet, Francis Ledwidge and Donaghmore, Co. Meath man, Matt McGoona. Before Ledwidge joined the British Army they were always together, and even shared an old rattling motor bicycle.

One evening in 1917, Matt was in the office of the 'Meath Chronicle' where he worked as a printer, when he heard in the distance the unmistakable noise of the old motor cycle and thinking that his friend, Francis had arrived home unexpectedly from the Front, dashed out to meet him. There he was – in his well-worn motoring suit – advancing with hands oustretched to greet his friend.

Matt, overjoyed, hurried forward to him, but then to his horror and dismay, the figure of Ledwidge suddenly disappeared into the shadows. A few days later a telegram arrived to say that Ledwidge had been killed about the same time that Matt had seen his figure. Matt McGoona lived another thirty years and his friends often heard him relate this story.

Monk appeared

Miss C. MacMullen Tivy of Adambeg sent me the following stories: 'There were two strange occurrences which took place in my family many years ago. The first happened to a Protestant Dean of Cloyne, the Rev. William Wilson, a distant cousin of my own. One night in the Deanery a Monk appeared to him. No cummuncation passed between them but the spirit remained long enough to his wondering sight for the Dean to take full cognisance of his demeanour and the order to which his habit belonged.

'The other happening took place at a much earlier period. My great grand-uncle, John Radcliffe of Holly Hill, Kinsale, was with thirty-five others blown up at the storming of Cape St. Vincent in 1780. On the night of his death his father saw the curtains of his bed drawn aside, and his son, John, standing beside him. In terrible agitation he woke his wife and told her what he had seen, and had the strength of mind to note the date and hour in his tablets.

'Six months later he received the news that on that date, and at that hour John had met his death.'

Phantom billiards contest

'During the piping days of the Emergency (1939–45),' writes H.M.B. of Rochfortbridge, Co. Westmeath, 'many large country residences in Co. Westmeath were taken over by the Army for the billeting of troops. I was an officer in a unit which moved in to occupy one such residence in 1940 and I happened to be rostered as Orderly Officer on the first day.

'That evening when I had attended to my normal routine duties I relaxed with a book before a nice fire

73

in the large room on the first floor being used as the Orderly Officers' quarters.

'The house and surroundings were then very quiet as the entire unit with the exception of those detailed for quard, "Stand-to" and fire picket duties had all left the camp to get acquainted with their new locality and its residents. As I was about to uick up the threads of the story which I was reading I was interrupted by the unmistakeable sounds of a game of billiards or snooker being played in another room across the corridor.

'As I was unaware that our new home possessed such an amenity as a billiards table I went across the corridor immediately to investigate.

'Imagine my dismay when I opened the door and found that the room was in complete darkness and, as I found on switching on the light, devoid of any furniture whatsoever. I was inclined to treat the whole thing as an aural illusion but I soon changed my mind, when, on closing the door, I again heard the same unmistakeable sounds of billiard balls clicking and tapping against each other, the sound of their falling into the pockets of a billiards table and even the gentle sound of chalk being applied to the tips of the cues.

'I listened for about five minutes, and then the tapping of the balls ceased suddenly, and I heard a sound as if a billiards cue was being flung with violent force against the ground. After that there was complete silence.

'At least one other member of our unit heard this eerie game being played during the first week of our occupation. After that – although it had no connection with our experience – the rooms mentioned were used as a quartermaster's stores, and so the ghostly player or players were never likely to be heard or interrupted after 4.30 p.m.'

Famine tragedy echo

'In the early part of 1908 I was staying on holidays with relations near Strokestown, Co. Roscommon,' writes Mr. J. S. B. of Lanesboro, Co. Longford. 'One day one of my aunts arrived home breathless and excited at about ten p.m. and began to tell my grandparents about something she had seen down the road.

'I was then about five years of age and was sent off to bed immediately, my aunt being admonished for "frightening the child with such nonsense".

'The incident remained vivid in my mind as I sensed with a child's unerring accuracy in such matters that there was something unusual about my aunt's story which I was not allowed to hear. About twelve years later when I was on a visit to my aunt I asked her what she had seen on the road that night in 1908 and she told me the following story:

"After the Famine of 1847 it was customary for intending emigrants from that part of Co. Roscommon to walk to Kilashee, Co. Longford where they boarded the canal barge for Dublin on the first stage of their journey overseas. Each emigrant tried to bring with him as much oaten meal or oaten bread as would suffice to keep him alive until he reached his destination.

"One intending emigrant named Sean Burke from a place called Rossaun had no provisions whatever to take with him and he visited a certain house in a near-by townland where he knew there was a plentiful supply. Despite his pleading, the owner of the house refused to give him anything except in exchange for a large round flagstone which was in Burke's house, and which would be useful, it appears, for the grinding of corn.

"Burke returned to his own home and despite his hunger and exhausion proceeded to carry the flagstone to the home of its new purchaser. However, the effort was too much for him and he fell under its weight on the way and died from hunger and exhaustion on the roadside.

"His spirit still returns at certain times and his ghost can be seen walking this road with his shoulders bent under the weight of a large object which he carries. When it reaches a certain hill the spectre appears to fall on the side of the road and disappears."

'This was the apparition which my aunt claimed she saw on that night. The hill in question she told me was always known in her youth as Thashy Woorky Hill (The Hill of Burke's Ghost).'

In Dungannon

According to reports in the 'Belfast Telegraph' in April, 1963 inhabitants of Dungannon were terrified by the ghost of Gallows Lane. This was said to be 'a tall man with a castor hat and staring eyes'. Weird unearthly cries were heard and a motorist saw the figure in the lights of his car.

Residents believe the ghost was a spirit of an eighteenth century shop stealer who was dragged along the lane to the gallows two hundred years ago. Tradition has it that people sentenced to death at the Assizes House at Market Street were forcibly led along the laneway and hanged on a tree at Gallows Hill.

Slieve Donard

Slieve Donard, the highest peak in the Mourne Mountains was the scene of a great annual pilgrimage up to the latter half of the nineteenth century. The mountain is called after St. Domanagart, a disciple of St. Patrick who was said to have founded a monastery at the foot of the mountain and often climbed up to the top to do penance.

The saint was reputed by the local people to be the mountain's perpetual guardian, and was reported to say Mass every Sunday on one of the cairns on the top. One legend told of a subterranean passage which ran from the shore near Newcastle to the summit. Some men found the entrance and ventured in. They were met by the stern figure of the saint in his robes. He rebuked them, and told them it was his own special residence until the Day of Judgement.

Clondalkin

The ghost of a monk was said to haunt the former Carmelite Monastery in Clondalkin. A young novice going down the corridor one night passed a monk, whom, he recollected later, he did not recognise as a member of the community. When he mentioned the occurrence next morning, a fellow-monk said, 'Oh, that's alright it was only Brother "X". His ghost often comes around, but he's quite harmless.'

Coolmoney House

Coolmoney House in the Glen of Imaal is used by the Army's Artillery Corps whose range lies close by. The house is said to be haunted by the spirit of a young woman who many years ago jumped to her death from one of the upstairs windows. It is said that few officers volunteer to sleep in this room, and some who did spent only one night there.

Monaghan

The ghost of an apostate priest is said to haunt the Monaghan roads. Sir Shane Leslie tells me the story was told to him by Dinny Rushe, secretary to the Local Council, who saw the apparition several times. Each time Dinny had a Mass said for the priest's soul. He had found the name in the old records as receiving a pension from the Government but would never reveal it.

CHAPTER 9

A voice from space and other strange stories

Voice from space

A Co. Limerick television viewer had an amazing experience in 1959. On his set he heard the voice of a man who had been dead for two years! The voice announced that the speaker was going to a dinner as a committee member of a certain boat club and had only one hour to dress.

It was part of a 'ham' radio broadcast between two friends, and on subsequent enquiry, the listerner, Mr. Charles Stewart of Patrickswell discovered that the man whose voice he had heard had been dead for two years.

'Apparently what I picked up was part of a broadcast he was making to another "ham",' says Mr. Stewart. 'His transmission must have travelled a long way in space and returned to earth having been bounced off a planet. It was uncanny.'

Radio experts did not accept Mr. Stewart's explanation, however. One of them said at the time that if it was the dead man's voice Mr. Stewart heard, the explanation could only be found in the realms of the occult. 'It was a ghost voice,' he said. Since then Mr. Stewart has read many letters from people abroad who read the account in the newspapers. They all had somewhat similiar experiences or had heard of such experiences from friends of theirs.

One correspondent from North Wales told him that several friends of his had received perfect reception of a Texas television station on one particular occasion even though the station in question had stopped transmitting and had gone out of existence two years previously. This was also verified by other correspondents.

Another letter – from England – told of a Mayday message being received from the Captain of a Comet airliner two years after the plane had crashed and despite the fact that it had been stated at an enquiry that no Mayday message had been received from the Cockpit.

The latter story was featured in the Reader's Digest and centred on the time after the war when there were a number of Comet crashes.

Stewart's theory, is that all this business of pictures and messages being received years after being transmitted may be caused by them fading into space at the time of transmission, 'bouncing' on distant planets and returning to earth to be picked up again by television, or perhaps radio sets.

He adds that his theory gains ground after the discovery in the past few years that television pictures and messages could be bounced off satellites and planets (e.g. Telstar). His own particular experience took place, Stewart also pointed out, when Sun spot activity was at a peak and this may have caused strange things to happen.

Seymour and Neligan tell of a former Lord Tirawley who was a wild and reckless man. 'One evening, it was said, when the nobleman was preparing for a night's carouse, a carriage drove up to his door, a stranger asked to see him, and, after a long private conversation, drove away as mysteriously as he had come. Whatever words had passed between them they had a wonderful effect on the gay lord, for his ways were immediately changed, and he lived the life of a reformed man.

'As time went on the effect of whatever awful warning the mysterious visitor had given him wore off, and he began to live a life even more wild and reckless than before. On the anniversary of the visit he was anxious and gloomy but he tried to make light of it. The day passed, and at night there was high revelry in the banqueting hall. Outside it was wet and stormy, and just before midnight the sound of wheels were heard in the courtyard!

'All the revelry stopped; the servants opened the door in fear and trembling; outside stood a huge dark coach with four black horses. The "fearful guest" entered, and beckoned to Lord Tirawley, who followed him to a room off the hall. The friends, sobered by fear, saw through the door the stranger drawing a ship on the wall; a piece of the wall then detached itself and the ship grew solid, the stranger climbed into it, and Lord Tirawley followed without a struggle. The vessel then sailed away into the night, and neither it nor its occupants were ever seen again.'

Boyne Valley

The same authors tell of a strange legend about a house in the Boyne Valley. The occupant of the guest chamber was always awakened on the first night of his visit, when he would see a pale light and the shadow of a skeleton 'climbing the wall like a hugh spider'. It used to crawl out on to the ceiling, and when it reached the middle would materialise into solid bones, holding on by its hands and feet; it would then break into pieces, and first the skull, and then the other bones would fall on the floor and disappear.

Near Clogheen

A lady in Clonmel, who wishes to remain anonymous, sent me several stories of which the following is worth including: 'On the Knockmealdown mountains overlooking Clogheen, Co. Tipperary there is a big pond which is said to be bottomless. Every Christmas morning at three a.m. a monster is said to come up out of this pond. It has the shape of a horse, with a woman's head, and it asks three times: "when will the Day of Judgment come?" and disappears.

'A woman known as Petticoat Lucie is also said to haunt the pond. One night a local man was going home this way, when a woman dressed in white came and sat on his car. The horse refused to pull the car, and after a while the man was knocked off and the horse, cart and woman shot off into the darkness. Next day he found the horse grazing peacefully on the hillside.

'The fairy tree that John McCormack sang about is only a short distance outside Clogheen and Katie Ryan who is mentioned in the song died not so long ago in Cashel Hospital.

'Kiltinan Castle, between Clonmel and Fethard got its name because a bishop or priest called Tinan lived in it. He was murdered by Cromwell's soldiers, and marks of the blood can be seen on the steps.'

Wexford's fairy rath

When extending one of the E.S.B. rural electrification schemes in the Whitechurch area of Co. Wexford in 1955, workmen found that one of the poles to carry cables had to be set up in the middle of a large fairy rath in a field belonging to Mr. J. Whitty of Wilkinstown.

The E.S.B. poles run in a straight line across the country-side, up hill and down dale, and are spaced equally apart. The men found that the pole in the rath gave them endless trouble because no matter how firm they made the earth around it the pole was found to be loose next morning.

Finally they made the hole six feet deep and rammed home the earth so that nothing could shake it, as they thought, but next morning it was as loose as ever. As a final effort they took it up and planted it four feet outside the rath, and since then it stands as firm as a rock.

The oldest folk tales are concerned with these fairy raths, rings of earth usually planted with hawthorns that are seen here and there throughout the countryside from time immemorial, and connected with each one is a story of how someone at some time or another tried to cut the bushes or dig away the clay bank and met with 'misfortune' while so engaged.

In recent years, however, since farms have become mechanised, some farmers have defied the old superstitions and have cleared away the raths although historical societies and individual antiquarians have pleaded to have them left as memorials of the past.

People who believe in the fairies find it amusing to think that the age-old mysterious little folk should win their battle to safe-guard their rath against the E.S.B., the representatives of this progressive age.

Witch of Bealaha

While engaged in widening a river at Bealaha, Co. Clare in 1955, Council workmen found a timber box and two bread knives embedded in the river bank. When the box was opened, it was found to contain two briar pipes and two open razors all in a fairly good state of preservation.

Believing that the objects may in some way be connected with a witch reputed to have her abode under one of the arches of the river bridges, the workmen destroyed the objects. There is a strong local tradition that in the 1820's there was a witch in the locality who came from under the bridge after midnight and attacked and killed with a knife any person passing over the bridge.

84

One night a man travelling on horse-back to summon a priest for his sick wife was attacked by the witch who jumped behind him on the horse but the man fore-warned of the danger struck first with his knife and then fell to the ground.

She then asked the man to pull the knife and stick it again, but he knowing that it would be as much as his life was worth if he did so replied: 'You have it now and keep it.' He then rode off on his horse and the next morning all that was found on the roadside was a lump of jelly with a knife stuck in it.

The find of the knives, pipes and razors aroused a good deal of curiosity in the district, and while some would like to believe that they were the property of the Witch of Bealaha the view held by the majority is that they were placed there at some time by a super-stitious person to ward off some evil as even up to the present day people in many parts of West Clare believe in witches and fairies.

CHAPTER 10

The Theatre

Micheal MacLiammoir's story

Here is the ghost story which I was told many years ago by that great man of the theatre, Micheal Mac-Liammoir. He wrote it down specially for me and I had the added pleasure of hearing him read it in that wonderful melodious voice of his –

It was in London in the year 1916: a month or so before the Easter Rising. A very young boy, yet I was an experienced professional: I had been on the stage for nearly six years! And among my many grown-up friends – stage children are often more at home with adults than with each other – was an English actor I will call Kenneth Dane, though only the first name was his own.

A good actor, a French scholar, an ardent convert to the Catholic Church, an enthusiast about all things Irish, and a friend of Mabel Beardsley, the sister of the great artist. Altogether an interesting, companionable and charming man, who, although he was scarcely thirty, seemed to me almost middle-aged and an authority on all things under the sun.

On account, I suppose, of his Catholic faith, he was given a commission in an Irish Regiment of the British Army – we may as well call it the Munster Fusiliers – though he had never set a foot in Ireland in his life and on this chilly week-end of early spring in 1916 (he was in England for a few days' leave) he and I met at a week-end party in a lovely Georgian house on the river near Richmond.

The party was gay, noisy and sentimental with an atmosphere of 'let us be merry for to-morrow we die' after the manner of the times. Kenneth and I shared the bedroom lit by candles and lamps: electricity had not yet penetrated to the suburbs, and on the third night of our stay, as we were preparing for sleep, he said to me: 'Do you ever get premonitions? I do. I know, for example, that I'll never see you – any of you – on this earth again, because I'm going to be killed, ye see. Oh, yes, I'm quite certain of it. In fact, I could say "I know." '

My head at this period of my life was much more filled with ghost stories than with sentiments of friendship and my thoughts expressed themselves – as is the habit with my thoughts – immediately. 'Promise me,' I said, 'that if you do get killed you will come and tell me so.'

Suddenly he looked at me over the candlelight that separated our two beds. I was smoking my first cigarette and I was immensely proud of it. He stubbed his out on an ashtray 'I'll come if God allows me – I'll come and tell you.'

I slept, youthful, heartless, and untroubled. When I woke next morning the bed next to mine was empty: his books, his clothes, his shaving things: all had been taken away, there was a faint smell of brilliantine in the air, that was all. And less than a week later, we received the news! He had been killed three days after his return to France.

Here I must repeat: I was youthful, heartless, and untroubled. No ghost had come to me: no message from the dead had arrived, no premonition had touched me, there had been no sign. And, as the years went by, in spite of our youthful vows of eternal friendship, I confess I forgot all about him.

It was twenty years later – in 1936 – that Hilton Edwards and I, who some eight years previously had established the Dublin Gate Theatre and done most of our early work, were sharing a flat in a certain street that had a church like a pepper-pot at the end of it. It was early Spring weather, dark, gloomy, and ominous: we had engaged a new manservant, unknown to us but for his references from Trinity College and an admission – or was it boast? – that he had once served in the British Army. He was interviewed and I felt he would be satisfactory.

'Don't knock on the door when you come up in the morning at nine,' I told him: 'Just bring in the coffee, open the curtains, and that will wake me.'

'Yes, sir.'

Next morning, although after our heavy work in the theatre I sleep well as a rule, I awoke long before nine. I was vaguely disturbed: I wondered why, and finally concluded that it was because of the new man. Would he burn our trousers as he pressed them as his predecessor had done? Would he fill the bath to overflowing, make the coffee all wrong? Presently I heard him coming up the stairs, a church clock somewhere was striking the hour of nine, I remember thinking: 'He's punctual, anyway.'

The door opened softly and a British officer entered

the room carrying a coffee tray.

I stared. The room was still dim with its drawn curtains and faint wintry light outside, but I could see him plainly. I thought: 'What is a British officer doing in Dublin in 1936?'

The man advanced into the room, and I saw that it was Kenneth Dane. In spite of the twenty years that had passed by since he died, there was no mistaking the spare figure: the light brown, smoothly-brushed hair: the lean, clean-shaven face. I almost shouted in my astonishment: 'Kenneth! Kenneth Dane!' And it was only then that I remembered his promise to me when I was a boy, and I said: 'You have come back to see me – after all!'

He nodded his head gravely: his lips, half smiling, moved as if in speech, but I heard no sound. He came close to the bed, set down the coffee tray on the table, and still with that old smile on his moving lips, still watching me intently, he turned and opened the curtains.

As the grey morning light streamed into the room, then that khaki-clad figure of the officer seemed to melt rapidly into that of a middle-aged, slightly stooping man: grey haired, and dressed in black trousers and a white linen coat. It was the new servant.

That was the only moment, I think, in which I felt any dismay. I gasped and almost wept, full of a strange, remote anguish: but, seeing the man staring at me in amazement, I made an effort, and muttered some foolish thing about a dream. But the servant's face was white.

'Excuse me, sir: but did you not call me Kenneth

Dane, just now when I was coming in?'

'I did, yes... I'd been dreaming about a very old friend of mine...'

'Excuse me, sir: but it wouldn't be Captain Kenneth Dane, sir, would it?'

'Yes. He was an army man. Why do you ask?'

'It wouldn't be Captain Dane of the Munster Fusiliers, sir? Would it?'

'Yes, that was his Regiment. Why?'

'But I was his batman, sir. I was with him in France in 1916 when he got the bullet that killed him. Captain Dane, he died in my arms, sir.'

After the curtain has come down at night and the players, stage hands and staff have gone home, a theatre is the eeriest place imaginable. If one stands on the empty stage it is easy to imagine that there is a phantom audience sitting watching out in the darkness, or if one looks up from the auditorium towards the stage it is easy to imagine the shades of some great actors of the past silently enacting again their moments of glory.

One of the few stories I have heard about a theatre happened in daylight, Maire Ni Dhomhnaill, the Abbey actress, tells me that when she first joined the company she was taking part in a dress rehearsal. During a lull she went into the stalls to sit down in one of the seats for a rest. After a while she suddenly felt someone brushing against her. She automatically stood up to let the person pass her, but to her amazement there was no-one there!

Later she told the story to some senior members of

the company. The late Maureen Delany asked where was the seat located. On being told she said: 'Sure that was where Lady Gregory used to sit, you should never sit there, child.'

It appears that when Lady Gregory was alive she resented anyone sitting in her favourite seat (third row from the stage, second seat in). After her death, whenever any member of the company sat in this seat during rehearsal they felt some presence pushing against them. People who sat there during a performance reported similar experiences.

Fishamble Street

The other story I heard about a theatre goes back 100 years and was told to me by M. A. D. of Clontarf: 'As a child I often heard my grandfather, John Hogan (1816–1898) tell us of a ghostly experience he had when he was apprenticed to a builder who was doing some repairs to the Fishamble Street Theatre. He was put to sleep in the Green Room, and every night exactly at ten p.m. a knocking came to the wall and continued for fifteen minutes.

'My grandfather was very frightened and asked to be allowed to sleep in another room, but he could not manage this, so all he could do was to pull the clothes over his head till the knocking stopped. A short while before his death he brought in a newspaper which stated that the theatre was about to be pulled down, and that it was supposed to be haunted, as every night for more than sixty years, a knocking had been heard in the Green Room from 10 – 10.15 p.m., but apparently no one had ever investigated further.'

The Fishamble Street Theatre was originally Mr. Neale's Music Hall, which opened in 1741. It became famous in that in April of the following year Handel's 'Messiah' had its first performance there 'for the relief of the prisoners in the several gaols and for the support of Mercer's Hospital... and of the Charitable Infirmary.'

In County Kerry

Some friends of mine had the following experience while touring Ireland a few years ago with a production of 'Night Must Fall' (writes Teddy Aherne, London). They were appearing in a parochial hall in a town in Kerry, and learned on arrival, that it had formerly served as a place of worship, a new church having been recently opened. The stage was situated where the altar used to be, and the men's dressingroom was directly behind it.

On the last night of their successful visit, the male members of the cast remained behind till the early hours of the morning to pack the scenery etc. as they had a long journey to the next venue, and when the work was finished, they all retired to the dressingroom for a smoke.

Suddenly in the deathlike stillness, they were all startled to hear quite distinctly the strains of an organ playing in the hall, and the shuffling of feet as if a large crowd was entering, and they had no idea of how long they listened to the eerie happenings. They were only conscious of finding themselves out in the street scurrying as fast as they could to their digs, and each of the four men related it exactly for a long time afterwards.

Experience of Maire Ni Dhomhnaill

The well known young actress of the Abbey Theatre Company, Maire Ni Dhomhnaill had an unusual experience during the company season in Belfast in 1954. Here is the story as she told it to me:

When we arrived in Belfast we put up in a small hotel a few streets away from the theatre, where we had been booked in. My husband, Geoffrey Golden and myself got a room on the third floor. Just around the corner from our bedroom door were three steps leading to another room, occupied by four of the company's actors.

After our opening night we retired to bed. I was feeling lonely and upset because it was the first time I had been seperated from my three young children. I found I couldn't sleep. My husband was fast asleep beside me. It must have been about midnight that I suddenly heard a strange sound. I listened carefully.

I should mention that the bed was in a corner of the room almost against the wall which was the gable end of the hotel. I suddenly realised that the sounds I heard were footsteps... and the footsteps were coming around the bed towards my side. I distinctly heard them as they approached towards the top of the bed next the wall.

They appeared to stop beside me. Then very clearly I heard a voice with an Northern accent clearly say: 'She's in vaudeville now, in vaudeville, in vaudeville now!' After this there was silence. I sat up but could see no-one. Nothing else happened that night, nor did I myself have any other ghostly visitor for the rest of the stay.

Later during our stay in the hotel another member of the company had a strange experience. One night late after the show my brother-in-law, Eddie Golden, was chatting with my husband and myself in our room. In the room up the three steps another colleague was reading a book. The following morning at breakfast, as we all gathered around the big table in the dining room in the hotel, in came the colleague, looking white in the face.

'What's wrong with you?' someone asked.

'I saw a ghost last night,' he said.

This remark was greeted with laughter from everyone except Geoffrey and myself. We then asked him to tell us what happened.

'Well,' he said, 'I was sitting in bed reading while you were in the other room when I suddenly became conscious of someone's presence in the room. I looked up and saw a figure in a sports coat coming towards me whom I thought was Geoffrey Golden. As he came nearer I realised it was a stranger, and almost immediately the figure turned round, retreated, and to my horror went right through the locked door!'

On the last day of our season the woman who owned the hotel gave a party for us all after the show. When she had hospitably passed round plenty of sandwiches and cakes she sat down and relaxed. After a while she went over to a press, took out a photo album and started to show us the usual family groups. As we looked over her shoulder our colleague suddenly asked: 'Who is that?' pointing to the photograph of a young man in sports coat and flannel trousers.

'Why that was my eldest son,' the woman replied. 'He was killed in the blitz,' she said sadly, 'and he was just going to be married, too. His fiancee was in show business.'

'But that was the man I saw in my room the other night and whom I thought was Geoffrey,' said our colleague.

As I looked at the photo I realised there was a good likeness, and then another thought came into my mind. I had just been talking to the hotel owners youngest son, and I suddenly realised his voice sounded almost the same as the voice I had heard in the bedroom at the beginning of our stay.